Breaking Pride

TEARING DOWN WALLS
WALKING IN HIS GRACE

Heather Bixler

Becoming Press, LLC

Heather Bixler/Becoming Press, LLC
www.becomingpress.com

Cover Photo from Lightstock by Xtian Designs

eBook Design: Heather Bixler
Paperback Design: Heather Bixler
Cover Design: Heather Bixler

Ordering Information:
Quantity sales. Special discounts are available on quantity purchases by corporations, associations, and others. For details, contact the "Special Sales Department" at the website address above.

Scripture quotations are from The World English Bible.

Table of Contents

Introduction

The broken mirror on the cover of this eBook is a symbol of broken pride. When we look in the mirror we focus on our image, what we look like, or what we are wearing. Pride is very similar in that our focus is always on ourselves, what we want, how we feel, the need to be right, and the desire to prevent others from seeing our flaws.

Pride is often used as a way to protect our hearts and to hide the truth. Pride causes us to shut down and build walls.

Often we close our hearts off because we are hurt, angry, or afraid. We may say to our self that what we feel or think isn't really that important. Or we may keep our thoughts and feelings to our self out of protection or to try and keep the peace.

When we live in a world where we shut down our hearts, we become a person that is truly unable to walk a life in the Spirit.

Guarding our heart doesn't require us to build walls around our heart, it requires us to keep our heart soft towards God's word and those around us. If we are going to guard our hearts then we need to grow deeper in

God's word instead of walking around with a heart of stone filled with pride.

Pride is just a symptom of what is truly rooted in our heart. We may feel that our pride will protect us and keep us safe. But the only thing pride really does is hurt those around us. It prevents us from walking in the Spirit and growing in our relationship with the Lord.

There are three things that cause pride to build up in our heart:

1. The desire to protect.
2. The desire to defend.
3. The desire to be in control.

All three of these things are rooted in fear.

The only way to prevent pride from taking root in our heart and our life is to embrace a life filled with faith, understanding, and forgiveness.

I pray this eBook is a blessing to you and will help you to develop an authentic relationship with the Lord!

Something Beautiful

by Heather Bixler

I'm not humble person. I'm not a giving person. Often the words that come out of my mouth are harsh and un-caring, maybe even a little judgmental. I'm afraid of everything.

I try to control everyone and everything....this is what I see when I look in the mirror and I am being honest with me.

But when I realize my weaknesses I lean on God and I see.

Someone who is humbled by her weaknesses that will never go away.

I see someone who finds her peace in God and desires to give because God has been so gracious to her.

In front of me in the mirror there's a woman, and when she shares her wounds and the ugly truth about herself she expresses the beauty of God's grace through her words.

I see someone who has faith to go wherever God has called her to go because she trusts in Him.

CHAPTER ONE

Living Behind a Wall

For though Yahweh is high, yet he looks after the lowly; but the proud, he knows from afar. **Psalm 138:6**

Often when we live in our pride we find our self living behind a wall, missing out on opportunities to connect with others. We may even find our self believing the lies and negativity surrounding us.

When we live in our pride we are saying the lies are true. In my own personal journey I have built a wall of pride around myself because I began believing the lie that I was not good enough. So I began to hide behind this wall and never share my true self with others.

I would hide the fact that I was a writer or I wouldn't share the good news, or bad news, of my life with others. I believed that people either wouldn't care or they would judge me. By doing this I was embracing the lie that I wasn't good enough to be heard or seen was true.

One way I had to tear down the wall was to be vulnerable and Just Be. Me. I needed to learn to accept myself, flaws and all, before anyone else would. How can anyone accept the whole you if you are hiding behind a wall?

When we live behind a wall of pride we trap in the power of the Holy Spirit and keep out relationships. Neither of these options are Okay., Jesus came to this earth to accomplish the exact opposite. Jesus came to release the Holy Spirit out and draw each person into new relationship with Him.

When we live in our pride we remove our self from the presence of the Lord and we do not walk in the Spirit.

If we are going to accomplish the will of the Lord we need to tear down this pride and begin walking in the Spirit. We need to do what Jesus did, release the Spirit into the world and draw people closer to Him. It means we will be vulnerable and our weaknesses will be exposed for all to see, but through this they will also see the Lord's strength, grace, and mercy.

Life is not about getting others to like us, or becoming popular, it is about drawing others to Jesus. Jesus shines best when our weaknesses show. This is when others see HIS strength, not ours.

CHAPTER TWO

Breaking Pride Hurts

> Most certainly I tell you, unless a grain of wheat falls into
> the earth and dies, it remains by itself alone. But if it dies,
> it bears much fruit. **John 12:24**

As I began writing this eBook I had no idea it would hurt so much. Typing the words out about pride brought a deep sense of pain to my body. Often when we confront our pride there is a bit of turmoil rolling around in our mind. We desire to live a life for Jesus but to actually put it into practice, we begin to feel the sacrifice it is going to take in order to live out a life that is filled with humility and understanding.

Breaking pride hurts. It literally means denying our natural instincts in order to live out a life filled with the fruit of the Spirit.

Ever wonder what is keeping the fruit of the Spirit from surfacing in your life?

It's Pride

Our pride keeps us from breaking our pride. Our pride tells us we don't have pride issues. Our pride says it is fine to work hard and become comfortable in our own ability to accomplish whatever it is we desire to accomplish. Pride says we don't need anyone to help us. It says that we can obtain the fruits of the Spirit on our own.

When we are full of pride we often hide our flaws under a rug because we need to be perfect, especially if we are Christians and we are going to be a witness for Christ. Too often we don't even realize that our weaknesses can also be used to be a witness for Christ. Nobody can really relate to someone who is perfect.

Coming to the realization that we have a pride issue is the first step in breaking the barriers of pride in our life. But like I said - it hurts, physically and mentally. The only way we can break pride is through prayer, total devotion to God and His word, and through living an intentional life for the Lord.

Buried under all that pride is either a heart that is delighted in the Lord or one that is not. Our key to breaking this pride is a desire to walk in the footsteps of Jesus. Sometimes our pride may be so deep that it is difficult for us to get to a point where we desire God instead of whatever it is that consumes our heart.

First, we need to trust God and trust He is who He says He is. Sometimes our first step to breaking pride includes getting to know God more. God's character is what brings us closer to Him because we know He is different. *When we know His character we know we can trust Him.*

Second, we need to know that our trust and faith in Him is crucial when we are on this journey to breaking pride. The pain will feel unbearable at times, and when we are finally broken of our pride we will discover humility in our vulnerability. That is when we can cling to God, His word, and prayer.

CHAPTER THREE

Resisting Our Brokenness

Yahweh is near to those who have a broken heart, and saves those who have a crushed spirit. **Psalm 34:18**

We like to pretend we aren't broken. So often, we resist the reality of our brokenness to the point of resisting God. When we resist the fact that we are broken, then we resist God's beautiful grace in our life.

Our brokenness is the only thing leading us to God and His heart. When we take the path that is hard for us, we soon realize just how much we need Jesus in our life. If we aren't broken then we never recognize just how much we need Him, and if we don't know how much we need Him then our relationship with Him will be stunted.

We like to resist our brokenness through will power. We feel the guilt of unrighteous thoughts and deeds and try to hide them under a rug hoping that no one will notice. Or we shame ourselves with our words because a "good" fruitful Christian would never act or think those types of "things."

But the truth is as much as we need to resist the enemy we need to embrace our brokenness. When we resist our brokenness we are then allowing the enemy into our life and hearts simply because we are embracing our pride. You see pride is found hiding with all the lies we tell ourself and those around us. We tell our self these lies because we need to be a "good witness" to those around us that are not Christians. We put all this pressure on our heart and mind to be the good example through our thoughts and deed. But there really is no glory found in pride. We can't live as a witness for Christ if we are hiding the TRUTH.

> The Word became flesh, and lived among us. We saw his glory, such glory as of the one and only Son of the Father, full of grace and truth. **John 1:14**

Jesus lived for truth and grace, and was, in fact filled with truth and grace. To be a witness that is hiding behind lies only leads others to the one who is the father of all lies, and that is the enemy. If we are going to be a witness for Christ then we need to embrace the truth, and we most certainly need to embrace HIS grace! Without the truth of our brokenness ruling our heart we will miss out on living and walking in His grace.

So many of us think that a strong, good believer is one who has achieved it all. But the fact is we will never achieve anything if we aren't willing to embrace the truth. The body of Christ is filled with successful Christians that have nice head shots and fancy church buildings. We have been caught in a lie that says you have to look and act like you have it all together to be a successful Christian and a good witness. But really the only thing we can do in our own power to be a successful Christian and a good witness to others is to embrace our brokenness.

Once we embrace our brokenness we will learn to resist the enemy and His lies. We can't resist Him with a heart of pride, our pride needs to be broken. Once we are broken we will have the strength to resist whatever it is that is keeping us from walking everyday in the Spirit and in His grace.

CHAPTER FOUR

It's Kind of Like Exercise

if my people, who are called by my name, shall humble themselves, and pray, and seek my face, and turn from their wicked ways; then I will hear from heaven, and will forgive their sin, and will heal their land.
2 Chronicles 7:14

Recently, I started taking exercise classes to get healthy and also lose weight. This weight loss has been something on my heart for a very long time. When I finally realized that food was an idol in my life and that as long as I stayed where I was, I would never be able to fully receive the life God had planned for me, I finally made the commitment to God to lose the weight.

It wasn't an easy commitment to make because in my heart I thought I had already made this commitment before through determination and will power, and I had failed. I had resolved in my heart several times before that I was going to lose the weight. This time I finally realized I couldn't do it on my own, no matter what I did, and I had to give up in order to fully surrender to Him.

Giving up is one step in the process of becoming broken. In order for us to surrender our life to God we need to let go of whatever it is we are trying to control.

As I started exercise classes I felt like a fool. I could hardly do any of the moves and I was always taking water breaks. I read the scripture on the wall of the gym that said, "Through God all things are possible..." I often found myself saying, "Lord, help me!" during my workouts because that was the only way I could see myself finishing the class.

Being broken is kind of like exercise in that it pushes you to your limit and it breaks your body, but in that brokenness you come back stronger. Now, when I work out, I can feel my body getting stronger, but there are still times where a workout will bring me to tears because it is so hard for me to do. When I accomplish something now, I know that it never would have happened overnight. My success is a gradual process of being broken and building that strength back up.

When we work out, our strength could never be built up if we didn't surrender to do the exercise and if we didn't push ourselves.

We resist our brokenness because we want to BE STRONG, but little do we know that strength is obtained only through our brokenness, because where we are weak and broken we find God's strength to get us through.

CHAPTER FIVE

Resist the Enemy

But the fruit of the Spirit is love, joy, peace, patience, kindness, goodness, faith, - **Galatians 5:22**

Often when we accept Jesus into our life we are told that the Holy Spirit lives in us. Then we are taught what the fruits of the Spirit are, and we are also told in the Bible that you will know who someone belongs to by their fruit. But too often we may find ourself trying to achieve the fruit of the Spirit on our own and then we find ourself balled up in a pit of guilt because through our own efforts we will always fail.

Even so, every good tree produces good fruit; but the corrupt tree produces evil fruit. 18 A good tree can't produce evil fruit, neither can a corrupt tree produce good fruit. 19 Every tree that doesn't grow good fruit is cut down, and thrown into the fire. **Matthew 7:17-19**

We often think the fruits of the Spirit are achieved by sheer will power. But unfortunately what we do not realize is that this will to be more filled with the Holy Spirit is actually pride.

Walking in the Spirit takes absolute and complete surrender to God and His son Jesus. There is no other way we will achieve the fruits of the Spirit in our life except through total surrender to God. If we want to be filled with the Spirit then we need to remain humbled. We need to resist the enemy and all his lies, and we need to resist pride. We need to resist the urge to defend, protect, and control. Achieving the fruits of the Spirit do not come by doing, but instead come to us through embracing our brokenness and resisting the enemy.

- Love comes through resisting hate.
- Joy comes through resisting fear.
- Peace comes through resisting wrath.
- Patience comes through resisting control.
- Kindness comes through resisting rudeness.
- Goodness comes through resisting sin.
- Faithfulness comes through resisting lies.
- Gentleness comes through resisting the need to be right.
- Self-control comes through resisting the desire to control everyone and everything around you.

> Be sober and self-controlled. Be watchful. Your adversary, the devil, walks around like a roaring lion, seeking whom he may devour. **1 Peter 5:8**

We need to learn to resist the enemy in order to walk in the Spirit. Our pride can easily shroud the Spirit living within us, but our humility will reveal it through the fruits of the Spirit and hearts that desire to resist the enemy and resist pride.

CHAPTER SIX

Letting Go of Guilt

But he gives more grace. Therefore it says, "God resists the proud, but gives grace to the humble. **James 4:6**

Guilt is a huge weapon the enemy uses to keep us living in our pride. When we feel guilty about something, we hide behind our shame and in our shame we desire to protect, defend, and control.

Our guilt tells us we are not good enough and we shrink behind a wall. It's difficult to walk in the Spirit and live a life of faith if we struggle with our guilt, because when we feel guilty we lack confidence in God and the plans that He has set out before us.

Pride is covering our heart with a wall in order to protect and defend our self from being rejected and hurt. We would rather no one know us personally and intimately because we are ashamed. If we can convince our self that we have it all together, or that we are better than the next person, then maybe we can prove our self worthy of our blessings from God.

It's difficult to accept God's grace in spite of our sin. We look at His grace and our guilt automatically kicks in and says we are not "good enough." God doesn't want good enough, God wants our heart to be focused and delighted in Him.

We need to be willing to accept His blessings no matter what, and that requires us to become vulnerable. When we are no longer protected by our pride the wall comes down and everyone, is aware of our flaws. We feel naked just like Adam and Eve did in the garden after they had sinned. We want to quickly cover up our vulnerability and our sin because being vulnerable is not easy.

But we need to learn, just like Adam and Eve did, that God will cover us up with His grace. We may be vulnerable and naked before the world, but hiding behind a bush isn't going to change anything. God would rather we come out from behind that bush, covered up with His grace so we can continue to walk WITH Him. Then the world will see His grace instead of the flaws that are so clearly there.

The miracles that God can make happen are really amazing when we are finally vulnerable and walking in His grace. *Walking in His grace...* notice how it's not "standing" or "hiding" behind His grace. When we embrace our brokenness we move forward in His will for our life, with His grace, all the guilt and shame is gone. We need to remain covered in His grace, just like Adam and Eve, although they never went back to being able to walk freely the way God intended. But they continued to have His covering over them, just like we now can continue to have the covering of Jesus over our bodies as we walk freely in this world.

God didn't send His only Son to die on the cross so that we can hide behind our guilt, shame, and pride. He wants us to come out from behind that wall and live free. However we will need to learn how to become vulnerable and willing to rely on Him for our covering first.

I Was Better

doing nothing through rivalry or through conceit, but in
humility, each counting others better than himself;
Philippians 2:3

There was a moment in my life where I had thought my
experience had given me the opportunity to treat others
as though I was better than them. I wanted to be among
different groups of people and when I finally made it
into these elite groups I thought that maybe I was FI-
NALLY "good enough."

You see, in my heart I thought acceptance by certain
people meant I was good enough. Or that popularity
meant I was a great Christian. It was a rude awakening
to realize that these relationships were not genuine. I
judged others for not being like me or belonging to the
groups that I now belonged to, and for not having the
same beliefs as me. Through some crazy events I fell of
my pedestal and realized that I was wrong.

It's been a very long road for sure, but going through
this made me honestly face my pride. It was not easy.
My heart was even bitter towards God and everyone

else involved for a very long time. I felt betrayed by God because I thought I was serving Him and He let me down. It reminds me of the story of the prodigal son, but I was the son who was angry at the father for giving so much to the prodigal. I was mad at God for not allowing me to stay in my pride that said I was good because of what I did, what I had, and who I knew.

We all want to be a part of groups and want to be accepted. But when we put our self-worth into who we know and what we do then we are bound to get caught up in our own pride.

My heart still hurts at the thought of the people I had hurt in the past because of the pride I carried around in my heart. I thought I was better than them and I was sure to let them know it. But I wasn't better, and in the end I was humbled and the other person was exalted.

I have asked for forgiveness and I pray for reconciliation. Sometimes I still find myself thinking, "If this person just would accept me then maybe I will be good enough again." It is a vicious cycle, because now that I know I was wrong I question my worth.

Breaking pride requires accepting all of our flaws. If we live in guilt and shame, we will be sure to hide behind a wall of pride. It's easier to hide the fact that my flesh desires acceptance and that's where I place my worth instead of placing it with God. Instead, I'd rather bring it into the light, making myself vulnerable, revealing my weaknesses.

When we hide, we live in pride; when we are real, God will heal.

CHAPTER EIGHT

You Can't Tell Pride it's a Sinner

Pride goes before destruction, and a haughty spirit before a fall. **Proverbs 16:18**

You can't tell pride that it's a sinner or that it has done something wrong. When we walk in our pride we build walls to protect ourselves. We automatically go into defensive mode instead of a responsive mode.

You can't tell someone that they need a Savior when their heart isn't open to the fact that they have done anything wrong. It's unfortunate because when we block out the truth we also block out His grace. You can't experience God's grace without the truth and if you are walking in pride.

Pride provides us with a false sense of protection. If we don't know we are a sinner, or if we can defend ourselves to others and make them believe we have not sinned, then maybe we can erase the truth and the sin. But the reality is that we can never erase our sin. We can never hide behind a wall of pride because God sees all and knows all. The only way to truly clear our sin from our life and our conscience is through humility.

We need to get to a place where we are broken. Everyone who accepts the Lord into their life has been broken at some point in time. Once we experience brokenness we will find the humility to embrace the truth: that we are a sinner.

Being a sinner is not what defines you as a person. A sin is something that isn't God-honoring, something that keeps you from building a relationship with God, or something that hurts you or someone else.

Asking these three questions can help you identify whether or not what you are struggling with is keeping you from accepting God's grace and causing you to walk in pride instead of the Spirit:

- Can any GOOD come out of this?
- Is it hurting you, your marriage, your family, or someone else?
- Would you want this for your own children?

It is pride that keeps us from forming and building a relationship with God, not sin. God saves us while we are still sinners. We need to overcome pride in order to receive God's grace and mercy. If we can't even admit we are a sinner then we can't receive God's grace. It's that simple!

His grace and mercy is ALWAYS there. We just need us to choose to grab hold of it and embrace it.

CHAPTER NINE

Insecurity

"If you set your heart aright, stretch out your hands toward him. If iniquity is in your hand, put it far away. Don't let unrighteousness dwell in your tents. Surely then you shall lift up your face without spot; Yes, you shall be steadfast, and shall not fear: **Job 11:13-15**

When we feel insecure we often struggle with guilt, shame, and doubt. The guilt and shame comes from the desire to change our flaws and fix all that is broken within us. The doubt comes when we are afraid to reveal the true person hiding beneath all that pride.

The pride protects our insecurities by building a wall around our heart and our thoughts, not allowing anyone in or letting anything out. Insecurity is the filter for the words that come out of our mouth, and the actions we choose to take, before reaching the next person. Insecurity breeds pride and is built on the guilt that says what we "should" and "shouldn't" feel.

When we hide out of insecurity we block people out. No one trusts a person that is hiding something, but we are afraid to reveal all that is within us because that means we need to be vulnerable, and the truth will be there for all to see. No more hiding behind a wall, the good, bad, and ugly will be laid out on the table for others to either accept or reject.

Nobody likes to be rejected. That's why we started hiding in the first place. The rejection is too painful to bear; it is a little easier to deal with the self-imposed isolation than the rejection, so we opt for the isolation instead. We may think perfection will obtain the acceptance we so desire. But how can others accept us if we don't accept ourselves, flaws and all?

Pride says we can be perfect. Pride says if we just do x, y, and z, then people will like us. SO we continue to hide our true self all the while working to be what everyone else wants us to be and we lose a little bit of our self every time we wallow in the guilt and shame of who we truly are.

In our efforts to try and fix who we are, by trying to move past our flaws with sheer will power, we build a false image of ourself to others, and we build false relationships, not only with friends and family, but also with God.

The only way to move past the guilt, shame, and insecurity is to truly accept who we are. We need to be real with our pain, to stop trying to change it and bring it into the light. Confess it to the Lord and simply accept it.

Nobody is perfect. If we are going to break our pride then we need to get the plank out of our own eye. But pride would rather take the focus off ourself and focus on the speck in our brother's eye. It's so much easier to judge and criticize the flaws of others because they are not our flaws. If we were to truly be honest with who we truly are, we would have no other choice but to move closer to God and begin to rely on Him.

Pride is self reliant, judgmental, and critical; it is also afraid and insecure. Pride just wants to protect itself from the pain of rejection, it just wants to be accepted and loved. But pride doesn't realize that acceptance and love comes from trusting God wholly and completely. The love and acceptance comes from surrendering our flaws to God instead of trying to hide them from Him, ourselves, and the ones we love. God accepts who we are, we need to learn how to accept ourselves completely.

Breaking Pride

Have this in your mind, which was also in Christ Jesus, who, existing in the form of God, didn't consider equality with God a thing to be grasped, but emptied himself, taking the form of a servant, being made in the likeness of men. And being found in human form, he humbled himself, becoming obedient to death, yes, the death of the cross. **Philippians 2:5 - 8**

To break our pride we need to let go of the control that consumes us. We need to let go of the desire to portray a certain image to those around us. We need to be willing to be vulnerable and open to those around us.

As we learn to leave our pride behind we will begin to form authentic relationships with our friends and family, and also with God. It's not our sin that keeps us from truly delighting in Him, it is our pride.

We try to cover up our sin because we know that our sin is a reflection of where our heart is towards God. We avoid church and the Bible because we simply do not want to change or let things go, that we love more than God. We don't want to admit we are wrong because we are hanging on to our pride, and we hang on to our pride so that we can be right.

The reality of life isn't made up as we go along. The reality of life has been the same reality since Adam and Eve were created in the garden. Just because we have been given free will doesn't mean that our actions are right, and it doesn't mean there aren't any consequences to those actions.

We know in our heart when we are wrong and we know when we are living in sin, but pride is the thing that keeps us from addressing this sin and letting it go. We also know in our heart the person we were designed to be, and that there is a battle between the royalty in our blood and the flesh on our body. We know the purity of heart that we desire, but too often we cling to the guilt and shame that comes with our sin. Pride stops us from having to face that guilt and shame. But the blood of Jesus allows us to bring the reality of our sin to the light while also covering us with His grace.

How do we break our pride? Truth. Prayer. Grace.

Truth comes first. If we can't be real with the reality of our heart and sin, then we will never be able to move onto the next step because pride will tell us we have nothing to pray about, nothing to confess. Pride says we don't need any help because we are OK, and everyone, including God's word, is wrong. But the truth is we are not OK, nobody is. If we can't face that truth then we are still hanging onto pride.

Prayer comes second. Once we allow the truth of our sin to penetrate our heart we can then pray. Pray for the sin specifically, not just a "God I'm a sinner prayer help me." No, we need to pray specifically: "God I envy this person, help me." or "God I'm involved in an affair, help me." We also need to confess these specific sins to someone else. If we are going to have an authentic relationship with God then we need to be specific in our prayer and confessions. If we can't be specific it is because we are ashamed and filled with guilt, then we are still clinging to our pride...

Grace is third. The truth is this: grace is always there, it's always available for everyone. However we need to work through the first two steps to even begin to have a heart that is able to accept and receive God's amazing grace. Think about it, while you are living in your pride and covering your sin, God has already forgiven you. The only thing holding you back from receiving His grace is your pride. We don't have to be perfect to receive His grace, in fact if we were perfect we wouldn't need His grace. We just need to let go of our pride and embrace the truth.

It all seems so simple, but breaking pride is truly hard. Once we are able to move into a life where we receive His never ending gift of grace we will find the fruits of the Spirit. We will also find freedom.... Often we hang onto our pride to obtain freedom, freedom to do whatever it is our fleshly body desires. But the truth is we are never free when we are living in sin. God's grace is the only thing that can bring us true freedom.

About the Author

Heather is a mom of three, married to a firefighter, and she is a writer. She is passionate about sharing God's word in a practical and loving way.

He has said to me, "My grace is sufficient for you, for my power is made perfect in weakness." Most gladly therefore I will rather glory in my weaknesses, that the power of Christ may rest on me.- **2 Cor 12:9**

Follow Heather

- **Author Blog:** HeatherBixler.com
- **Twitter:** @hbixler03
- **Facebook:** HeatherBixlerWrites
- **Pinterest:** @hbixler03
- **Instagram:** @hbixler03

Audiobooks

If you like audiobooks then be sure to check out
Heather's audiobooks on audible and iTunes!

Reviews Needed!

I would love to hear your feedback - please leave your
reviews of *Breaking Pride* online wherever books are
sold!

More Resources

To view more practical Bible Studies visit:

http://becomingpress.com

Lead a small group: Join our free online leader training
and receive free resources for you to use in your Faith -
Four Week Mini Bible Study small group/Bible Study!

Learn more and sign up here:
http://becomingpress.com/leaders/

More Books by Heather

Be You – Four Week Mini Bible Study

Breaking Pride: Tearing Down Walls, Walking in His Grace

Desires of My Heart: Meditation on Psalm 37:4

Devotions for Moms: Thirty-Seven Devotionals

Faith – Four Week Mini Bible Study

Hope – Four Week Mini Bible Study

Love - Four Week Mini Bible Study

My Scripture Journal: Fearing the Lord

My Scripture Journal: Gratitude

My Scripture Journal: The Promises of God

My Treasures - Four Week Mini Bible Study

Rejected - Four Week Mini Bible Study

Worship is This - Four Week Mini Bible Study

Made in the USA
Columbia, SC
14 April 2021